babyknits
Hats & Booties

babyknits

Hats & Booties

15 Matching Sets for Noggins and Tootsies

Edie Eckman, Bonnie Franz & Debby Ware

Creative Publishing international

Chanhassen, MN

To LLL babies and moms everywhere — Edie Eckman
To my mom, who taught me how to knit — Bonnie Franz
To Owen and Will — Debby Ware

Creative Publishing international

Copyright 2006
Creative Publishing international, Inc.
18705 Lake Drive East
Chanhassen, Minnesota 55317
1-800-328-3895
www.creativepub.com
All rights reserved

President/CEO: Ken Fund
Executive Editor: Alison Brown Cerier
Executive Managing Editor: Barbara Harold
Senior Editor: Linda Neubauer
Photo Stylist: Joanne Wawra
Photo Art Director: Tim Himsel
Art Director: Brad Springer
Photographers: Steve Galvin and Joel Schnell
Production Manager: Linda Halls
Illustration: Deb Pierce
Book Design: Dania Davey

Printed in Singapore:
10 9 8 7 6 5 4 3 2 1

Library of Congress Cataloging-in-Publication Data
Eckman, Edie.
  Babyknits hats and booties : 15 Matching Sets for Noggins and Tootsies / Edie Eckman, Bonnie Franz, Debby Ware.
      p. cm.
    ISBN-13: 978-1-58923-274-7 (soft cover)
    ISBN-10: 1-58923-274-7 (soft cover)
   1. Knitting--Patterns. 2. Infants' clothing. I. Franz, Bonnie.
II. Ware, Debby. III. Title.
   TT825.E2915 2006
    746.43'20432--dc22
2005037536

All the yarns used in this book can be found or ordered at your local yarn shop or craft store. Visit the following web sites for more information about the yarns shown:

Coats & Clark
www.coatsandclark.com

Dale of Norway
www.dale.no

Kraemer Yarns
www.kraemeryarns.com

Lion Brand Yarn Company
www.lionbrand.com

Patons Yarns
www.patonsyarns.com

Plymouth Yarn Company
www.plymouthyarn.com

S. R. Kertzer Limited
www.kertzer.com

CONTENTS

Knitting Hats and Booties

There is nothing as precious as a baby. Who can resist the urge to top that adorable noggin and warm those tiny tootsies with a hand-knit hat and booties set? The pleasure of turning out something so charming in such a short time is positively addictive. Watch out—the cuteness packed into these pages will fuel your baby-knit habit!

This book is all about variety. Different looks just seem right for different babies, and so you need choices. Three designers have created sets with a range of looks from updated classic to total whimsy. You will find sets for girls, boys, or either one. Do you feel drawn to the pink lace bonnet with matching socks, or the fur-trimmed, *oo-la-la* beret? To the super-chunky ribbed hat, the updated argyles, or the set with the friendly "Sam the man" face? Flip through the pages and see all the possibilities!

While the hats and booties are knitted in many different stitch patterns, none of them is too difficult for even a beginner. Some are knitted in the round; others are knitted flat and sewn together. Some sets are knitted in plain, smooth yarns with interesting stitch patterns to create pebbly textures, ribs, lacy openwork, or cables.

Several sets use color patterning to create stripes, color blocks, even an argyle design. There are also a few projects that feature novelty yarns like fur, bouclé, and chenille. Each hat has matching booties that have the same style elements and that use the same yarns and techniques.

The instructions include the step-by-step pattern and information on the yarns, needles, notions, and gauge. For the yarns, there is both a generic description and the brand name and color shown, so you can knit an identical set or choose similar-weight yarn or a different color. Always knit a gauge sample before you start a new project. Yes, it will delay the fun part, but it's the smart approach and the only way to know you'll get the right size. Most of the hats and booties are sized to fit babies up to 12 months. Some yarns and stitches stretch more than others and, of course, baby heads come in different sizes. If the hat or bootie is a bit big at first, that's usually just fine.

The instructions are easy to follow, and there are extra photos to show you the stitches and details up close. Some techniques that may be unfamiliar to you are explained in more detail in the back of the book. There, too, you will find a list of abbreviations.

Enough small talk, let's get to the good stuff. Pick out a few projects, head to the yarn shop, and start knitting hats and booties for the little one in your life. Bet you can't knit just one!

Roly-Poly Ridges

Design by Bonnie Franz

This simple-to-knit hat is the perfect first project to work in the round. The gentle roll of the brim is stopped with ribbing, which helps keep the hat on the baby's head! Garter ridges add both color and texture.

Roly-Poly Ridges

Size: 12 to 18 months
Head circumference:
16" (40.5 cm)

YARN

3 LIGHT Lightweight smooth yarn
(A): approx 90 yd (82.3 m),
(B): approx 15 yd (13.7 m),
(C): approx 40 yd (36.6 m),
(D): approx 8 yd (7.3 m)

Shown: Lion Brand *Baby Soft;*
60% acrylic, 40% nylon; 5 oz
(140 g)/459 yd (420 m):
1 ball each #920-176 Spring
Green (A), #920-156 Pastel
Green (B), #920-100 White (C),
#920-157 Pastel Yellow (D)

NEEDLES AND NOTIONS

One size 6 (4.0 mm) circular
needle 16" (40 cm) long, or
size needed to get gauge

One set size 6 (4.0 mm) dpns,
or size needed to get gauge

One pair size 6 (4.0 mm)
knitting needles, or size needed
to get gauge

Ten stitch markers, one in a
different color to mark beg of
rnd

One blunt-end yarn needle

GAUGE

20 sts and 28 rows = 4" (10
cm) over St st worked in the
round

Stripe sequence

(work twice)
K 5 rnds A, k 1 rnd B, p 1 rnd B, k 5 rnds C, k 1 rnd D, p 1 rnd D.

HAT

This hat is worked in the round. Switch to double-pointed needles when the stitches no longer fit comfortably on the circular needle.

Brim

With the circular needle and A, CO 80 sts. Join, being careful not to twist sts. Place a marker (pm) on the needle to indicate beg of rnd, and slip the marker every rnd. Knit 5 rnds, then work 2 rnds in k1, p1 rib. Begin the stripe sequence and inc one st on first rnd—81 sts. Work even in stripe sequence until piece measures 3½" (8.9 cm) from ribbing.

Crown

Continue with stripe sequence until it has been worked twice, then work in St st with A only.

Next (dec setup) rnd *K7, k2tog, pm; rep from * around—72 sts.

Next 2 rnds Work even in patt as established.

Next (dec) rnd *Knit to 2 sts before marker, k2tog, slip marker; rep from * around.

Rep last 3 rnds 5 times—18 sts.

Next rnd Knit.

Next rnd [K2tog] around, removing dec markers—9 sts.

Next rnd [K2tog] around, ending k1—5 sts.

Cut yarn, leaving a 6" (15.2 cm) tail.

Use a yarn needle to pull the tail through the rem sts twice, pull tight, and secure tail on WS.

Weave in all ends.

BOOTIES

Make two. These booties are knitted flat from sole up, then sewn together.

Sole

With A, CO 16 sts, pm, CO 1 st, pm, CO 16 sts. Knit 1 row—33 sts.

Inc Row K1, M1, knit to marker, M1, slip marker, k1, M1, knit to last st, M1, k1—37 sts.

Rep Inc Row twice more—45 sts. Remove markers.

Knit 3 rows.

Instep

Next 5 rows Beg with a RS row and cont with A, work in St st.

Next row (WS) P21, pm, p3, pm, p21.

Dec Row 1 Knit to 2 sts before marker, ssk, slip marker, k3, k2tog, knit to end—43 sts.

Dec Row 2 Purl to 2 sts before marker, p2tog, slip marker, p3, ssp, purl to end—41 sts.

Rep Dec Rows 1 and 2 three more times—29 sts rem. Remove markers.

Next 2 rows With B, knit. Break off B.

Next 5 rows With C, beg with a RS row, work in St st.

Next 2 rows With D, purl. Break off D.

Next 3 rows With A, purl 1 row, then work 2 rows in k1, p1 rib.

Next 6 rows With A, work in St st.

BO all sts loosely. Break off A, leaving an 8" (20.3 cm) tail for seaming.

Finishing

Fold the bootie in half and sew the sole and back seams.

Weave in all ends.

To make the tie, CO 100 sts with C, then BO all sts.

Using a yarn needle, weave the tie through the ridge at ankle on bootie (see photo); tie in a bow.

Stockinette stitch rolls toward the knit side to form the brim.

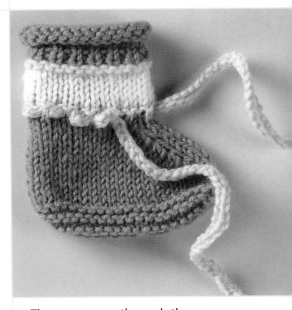

Ties are woven through the stitches at the ankle.

Grape Fizz

Design by Bonnie Franz

"Mistake stitch" ribbing gives great texture, but is simple and quick to knit. The drawstring design of the hat makes finishing easy. White edging adds the fizz.

Grape Fizz

Size: 12 months
Head circumference:
14½" (36.8 cm)

YARN

[3] Lightweight smooth yarn
(MC): approx 150 yd (137.2 m),
(CC): approx 8 yd (7.3 m)

Shown: Lion Brand *Baby Soft*;
60% acrylic, 40% nylon; 5 oz
(140 g)/459 yd (420 m):
1 ball each #920-143 Lavender
(MC) and #920-100 White (CC)

NEEDLES AND NOTIONS

One pair size 6 (4.0 mm)
needles, or size needed to get
gauge

Set of size 6 (4.0 mm) dpns, or
size needed to get gauge

One blunt-end yarn needle

One size G-6 (4.0 mm) crochet
hook (see note on ties)

GAUGE

25 sts and 30 rows = 4" (10
cm) over Mistake Rib

Mistake rib stitch pattern

(multiple of 4 sts + 3)
Row 1 *K2, p2; rep from * to last 3 sts, ending k2, p1.
Rep row 1.

HAT

This hat is worked flat and seamed.

Brim to crown

With CC, CO 91 sts. Work 1 row in Mistake Rib. Change to MC and work even in patt as established for 7" (17.8 cm).

Cut yarn, leaving a 6" (5.2 cm) tail. Use a yarn needle to thread tail through sts twice; pull tight and secure to WS.

Finishing

Seam the back of the hat.

Weave in all ends.

BOOTIES

Make two. These booties are begun flat, then worked in the round.

Cuff

With CC, CO 31 sts. Work 1 row in Mistake Rib. Change to MC and work even in patt as established until piece measures 2" (5.1 cm) from beg, ending with a WS row, and inc 1 st on last row—32 sts.

Heel flap

Slip sts to dpns as follows: place 8 sts on the first dpn; place next 16 sts on the second dpn (instep sts); place last 8 sts on the first dpn.

Next 11 rows Slipping the first st of each row pwise, work back and forth in St st on the 16 sts on the first needle only.

Turn heel

Row 1 (WS) Sl 1, p8, p2tog, p1, turn.

Row 2 Sl 1, k3, ssk, k1, turn.

Row 3 Sl 1, p4, p2tog, p1, turn.

Row 4 Sl 1, k5, ssk, k1, turn.

Row 5 Sl 1, p6, p2tog, p1, turn.

Row 6 Sl 1, k7, ssk, k1.

Gusset

Pick up and knit 6 sts along side of heel flap. With the free dpn, knit across 16 sts on second needle. With a third dpn, pick up and knit 6 sts along other side of heel flap, then cont across first needle—22 sts on first needle, 16 sts on second needle.

Rnd 1 Knit all sts.

Rnd 2 On the first needle, k1, ssk, knit across to last 3 sts, k2tog, k1; on the second needle, knit all sts.

Rep these 2 rnds until 32 sts rem—16 sts on each needle.

Next 7 rnds Knit.

Toe

Rnd 1 Knit all sts.

Rnd 2 On the first needle,* k1, ssk, knit to last 3 sts, k2tog, k1; rep from * on the second needle. Rep these 2 rnds until 12 sts rem—6 sts on each needle.

Graft sts together (page 93).

Tie

Using a crochet hook and CC, crochet a chain 15" (38.1 cm) long, leaving 4" (10.1 cm) tails at beg and end. Thread through ribs just above heel flap. Tie in a bow. *Note: If you don't want to crochet a chain, you could use ribbon or make a braid.*

Mistake rib is very stretchy.

Sock-stye booties have mistake-rib cuffs.

Sweet Lace

Design by Bonnie Franz

Nothing's sweeter on a baby than a lace bonnet. This set is particularly easy to make, because it is knit back and forth. Worked in white, it would make a wonderful christening set.

Sweet Lace

Size: 12 months
Bottom edge of bonnet:
approx 12³/₄" (32.4 cm)

YARN

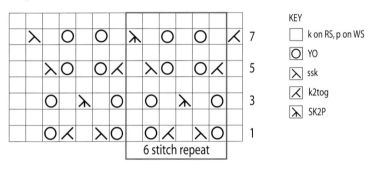 Lightweight smooth yarn:
approx 130 yd (118.9 m)

Shown: Lion Brand *Baby Soft;*
60% acrylic, 40% nylon; 5 oz
(140 g)/ 459 yd (420 m):
1 ball #920-103 Bubble Gum

NEEDLES AND NOTIONS

One pair size 6 (4.0 mm)
knitting needles, or size needed
to get gauge

Two stitch holders

Two stitch markers

One blunt-end yarn needle

GAUGE

20 sts and 30 rows = 4" (10
cm) over lace pattern

Lace Stitch Pattern

(multiple of 6 sts + 7)
Row 1 (RS) K1, *yo, ssk, k1, k2tog, yo, k1; rep from * to end of row.

Row 2 and all WS rows Purl.

Row 3 K1, *yo, k1, SK2P, k1, yo, k1; rep from * to end of row.

Row 5 K1, *k2tog, yo, k1, yo, ssk, k1; rep from * to end of row.

Row 7 K2tog, *k1, yo, k1, yo, k1, SK2P; rep from * to last 5 sts, ending k1, yo, k1, yo, k1, ssk.

Rep Rows 1–8.

KEY	
☐	k on RS, p on WS
Ⓞ	YO
⅄	ssk
⟋	k2tog
⅄	SK2P

6 stitch repeat

BONNET

This bonnet is worked flat and then seamed.

Front to back

CO 67 sts and knit 4 rows. Purl 1 row. Begin lace patt, and work until piece measures 4¹/₂" (11.4 cm) from beg, ending with a WS row.

Next row (RS) BO 24 sts, work in patt to end.

Next row BO 24 sts, work in patt to end—19 sts.

Work even in patt as established for 4" (10.2 cm). BO all sts.

Finishing

Sew bound off edges to sides of center portion to form bonnet.

Pick up 68 sts across bottom edge of bonnet. Knit 4 rows. BO.

Make two 3-st I-cord ties (page 91), each 11" (27.9 cm) long. Sew the ties to the edge of the bonnet.

Weave in all ends.

BOOTIES

Make two. These booties are worked flat, then seamed. For ease in working, a third needle can be used for the first several rows of the foot shaping; this can be a double-pointed needle if you choose.

Cuff

CO 25 sts. Knit 4 rows. Purl 1 row. Beg lace patt, and work even until the piece measures 2" (5.1 cm) from beg, ending with a RS row.

Instep

P8 and place these sts on a holder; p9; place rem 8 sts on another holder.

Work even in St st on center 9 sts for 2" (5.1 cm), ending with a RS row.

Foot

Next row (RS) Cont the previous row, pick up and knit 13 sts from the side of the instep strip, then knit across the sts on the holder; turn.

Next row Purl across all sts, pick up and purl 13 sts from the other side of the instep strip, purl across the sts on the second holder—51 sts.

Next row K25, place marker, k1, place marker, k25.

Work 9 rows even in St st, ending with a WS row.

Heel and toe

Row 1 K1, ssk, knit to 3 sts before first marker, k2tog, k1, slip marker, k1, slip marker, k1, ssk, knit to last 3 sts, k2tog, k1.

Row 2 Purl.

Rep rows 1 and 2 twice more.

BO all sts.

Finishing

Fold the bootie in half and sew seam.

Weave in all ends.

Open lace pattern makes a lightweight, delicate fabric.

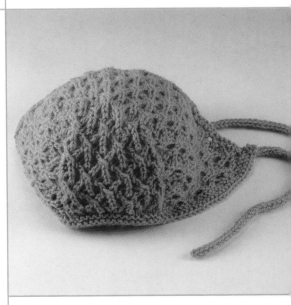

Front and lower edge are worked in garter stitch.

Baby's First Argyles

Design by Bonnie Franz

This traditional argyle-style pattern is created by knitting with two colors on each row—no bobbin hassles! The garter stitch flaps will keep baby's cheeks warm.

Baby's First Argyles

Size: 12 months
Head circumference:
15" (38.1 cm)

YARN

🔵 Lightweight smooth yarn
(MC): approx 120 yd (109.7 m),
(CC): approx 65 yd (59.4 m)

Shown: Lion Brand *Baby Soft;*
60% acrylic, 40% nylon; 5 oz
(140 g)/459 yd (420 m):
1 ball each #920-157 Pastel
Yellow (MC) and #920-176
Spring Green (CC)

NEEDLES AND NOTIONS

One size 5 (3.75 mm) circular
needle 16" (40 cm) long

Set of size 5 (3.75 mm) dpns

One size 6 (4.0 mm) circular
needle 16" (40 cm) long, or
size needed to get gauge

Eight stitch markers, one in a
different color to mark beg of rnd

One blunt-end yarn needle

GAUGE

26 sts and 23 rows = 4" (10
cm) over stranded St st using
larger needles

HAT

This hat is worked in the round. Switch to double pointed needles when the stitches no longer fit comfortably on the circular needle.

Brim

With the smaller circular needle and CC, CO 96 sts. Join, being careful not to twist sts. Place a marker on the needle to indicate beg of rnd, and slip the marker every rnd.

Work 5 rnds in k1, p1 rib. Change to the larger needle and begin the argyle pattern. Work even until the chart is complete. Break off CC.

Crown

Change to the smaller needle and cont using MC only.

Next (Dec setup) rnd *K10, k2tog, place marker; rep from * around—88 sts.

Next rnd Knit.

Next (Dec) rnd *Knit to 2 sts before marker, k2tog; rep from * around—80 sts.

Rep last 2 rnds 7 times—24 sts.

Next 2 rnds Work Dec rnd—8 sts.

Cut yarn, leaving a 6" (15.2 cm) tail.

Use a yarn needle to pull the tail through the rem sts twice, pull tight, and secure the tail on the WS.

Ties and Earflaps

Make two.

With the smaller needles and MC, CO 3 sts.

Work in garter st until the tie measures approx 12" (30.5 cm).

Next row K1, M1, k1, M1, k1.

Row 2 and all WS rows Knit.

Rows 3, 5, 7, 9 K1, M1, knit to last st, M1, k1.

Rows 10-16 K15.

BO all sts.

Finishing

Using a yarn needle and CC, sew the flaps to the bottom edge of the hat.

Weave in all ends.

Argyle stitch pattern

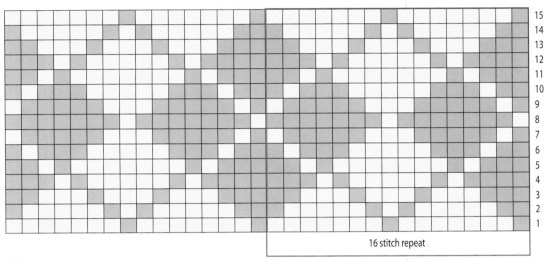

16 stitch repeat

KEY

☐ MC

▨ CC

Eight evenly spaced decrease locations form the gently rounded crown of the hat.

BOOTIES

Make two. These booties are knitted flat from sole up, then sewn together.

Sole

With larger needles and MC, CO 16 sts, pm, CO 1 st, pm, CO 16 sts—33 sts.

Knit 1 row.

Next (Inc) row K1, M1, k to marker, M1, slip marker, k1, M1, k to last st, M1, k1—37 sts.

Rep Inc Row twice more—45 sts. Remove markers.

Knit 3 rows.

Instep

Work 5 rows in St st, beg with a RS row.

Next row (WS) P21, pm, p3, pm, p21.

Dec Row 1 Knit to 2 sts before the marker, ssk, slip marker, k3, slip marker, k2tog, knit to end—43 sts.

Dec Row 2 Purl to 2 sts before the marker, p2tog, slip marker, p3, slip marker, ssp, purl to end—41 sts.

Rep Dec Rows 1 and 2 twice more—33 sts. Remove markers.

Next row K15, k2tog, k16—32 sts.

Leg

Change to the smaller needles and work the Argyle Chart.

Break off MC. Complete with CC only.

Next row Knit.

Next 5 rows *K1, p1; rep from * to end of row.

BO loosely in rib.

Finishing

Fold the bootie in half, then sew the sole and back seam.

Weave in all ends.

Rib, Rib

Design by Bonnie Franz

This reversible two-color Brioche hat is twice as warm and twice as colorful. The ribs are very stretchy, so a baby can wear this hat for a surprisingly long time. Choose sharply contrasting colors to make a bold statement, or go for a more subtle "shadow" effect by using more closely related hues.

Rib, Rib

Size: 12 months
Head circumference:
15" (38.1 cm)

YARN

[4] **MEDIUM** Medium weight smooth yarn (MC): approx 80 yd (73.2 m), (CC): approx 80 yd (73.2 m)

Shown: Lion Brand *Wool Ease;* 80% acrylic, 20% wool; 3 oz (85 g)/197 yd (180 m):
1 skein each #620-117 Colonial Blue (MC) and #620-102 Ranch Red (CC)

NEEDLES AND NOTIONS

One size 6 (4.0 mm) circular needle, or size needed to get gauge

Set of size 6 (4.0 mm) dpns, or size needed to get gauge

One blunt-end yarn needle

GAUGE

16 sts and 40 rows = 4" (10 cm) over Brioche st.

SPECIAL ABBREVIATIONS

sl 1 and yo Bring yarn forward and slip next st pwise. In working the following st, bring yarn over the top of the needle; a yo will be formed across the slipped st.

k1 tog with yo Insert the needle into the next st (which has a yo lying across it) kwise; knit the stitch and the yo together.

p1 tog with yo Insert the needle into the next st (which has a yo lying across it) pwise; purl the st and the yo together.

Two-color Brioche stitch pattern

(multiple of 2 sts + 1)
This stitch must be worked back and forth on a 2-ended needle, either circular or dpn. You will work across the sts first with one color, then, without turning the work, slide the stitches back to the opposite end of the needle and work the next row in second color. In other words, you will work two rows before turning your work.

Set up row With MC, p1, *p1, sl 1 and yo*; rep from * to last 2 sts, p2. Do not turn. Slide sts back to opposite end of needle.

Row 1 With CC, k1, *sl 1 and yo, k1 tog with yo; rep from * to last 2 sts, sl 1 and yo, k1. Turn.

Row 2 With MC, p1, *k1 tog with yo, sl 1 and yo; rep from * to last 2 sts, k1 tog with yo, p1. Do not turn. Slide the sts back to the opposite end of the needle.

Row 3 With CC, k1, *sl 1 and yo, p1 tog with yo; rep from * to last 2 sts, sl 1 and yo, k1. Turn.

Row 4 With MC, p1, *p1 tog with yo, sl 1 and yo; rep from * to last 2 sts, p1 tog with yo, p1. Do not turn. Slide the sts back to the opposite end of the needle.
Rep Rows 1–4.

HAT

This hat is worked flat and seamed.

Brim to crown

With MC, CO on 61 sts. Begin 2-color Brioche st, and work even until piece measures approx 7" (17.8 cm) from beg, ending with Row 4.

Next row With CC, k1, *k2tog with the yo; rep from * to end of row—31 sts.

Cut yarn, leaving a long tail.

Finishing

Use a yarn needle to pull the tail through the rem sts twice and pull tight.

Use the tail to sew the back seam.

Weave in all ends.

BOOTIES

Make two. These booties are begun at the cuff followed by the instep, both of which are worked flat; the foot is worked in the round.

Cuff

With dpns and MC, CO 21 sts. Work even in 2-color Brioche st for 18 rows, ending with Row 1.

Break off CC and complete with MC *only*.

Next row (RS) Knit across, knitting the yos tog with the sts they cross.

Next row Purl.

Next (eyelet) row K1, *yo, k2tog; rep from * to end of row.

Next row Purl. Break yarn.

Brioche stitch is very stretchy and warm.

Instep

Slip 3 sts from one end of the needle onto another dpn, then slip 4 sts from other end of the needle onto same dpn—7 sts on the new dpn.

Next 20 rows With MC, work back and forth in St st on these 7 sts *only*.

Next row (RS) K2tog, k3, k2tog; with second dpn, pick up and knit 10 sts along left side of instep; with third dpn, knit across 14 cuff sts; with fourth dpn, pick up and knit 10 sts along right side of instep—39 sts total.

Dominant color on one side becomes the "shadow" color on the reverse side.

Foot

Rearrange sts as follows:

Needle 1 (N1) 5 sts across toe

Needle 2 (N2) 15 sts along side

Needle 3 (N3) 4 sts across heel

Needle 4 (N4) 15 sts along other side

Knit 6 rnds.

Heel and toe

Rnd 1 *N1: Knit. N2: Ssk, knit to last 2 sts, k2tog. Rep from * on N3 and N4.

Rnd 2 Knit around.

Rep Rnds 1 and 2 twice more—27 sts total.

Finishing

Slip the sts from N1 onto N2, and sts from N3 onto N4—14 sts on N2, 13 sts on N4.

Fold the bootie in half and turn it inside out.

Seam the bottom by working 3-needle BO as follows: holding the two needles parallel with right sides together, use a third needle to k1 from N4; *knit together the next sts on each needle, then pass the first st over the second to BO; rep from * across, and fasten off last st.

Ties

Make two.

CO 70 sts with CC, then BO all sts.

Weave the tie through the eyelets, then tie it in a bow.

Weave in all ends.

Soft and Simple

Design by Edie Eckman

Who can resist a happy baby wearing a soft, plush hat-and-bootie set? This hat is super easy to make—it's just garter stitch! The booties are a sock mini-workshop; you can learn the basics of socks in an hour or less and have something for the baby when you are done.

HAT

Slip all stitches purlwise.

Brim to crown

Loosely CO 42 sts.

Work in garter stitch until the hat measures 7" (17.8 cm) from beg.

BO.

Finishing

Sew the side and top seams.

Pull the top corners to the center of the top seam and tack them together.

Weave in all ends.

BOOTIES

Make two.

Cuff

With dpns, loosely CO 16 sts. Place a marker on needle to indicate beg of rnd, and slip marker every rnd.

Rnds 1, 3 and 5 Knit.

Rnds 2, 4 and 6 Purl.

Heel flap

Worked on 8 sts only.

Rows 1-9 K8, turn.

Turn heel

Row 1 K4, ssk, k1; turn, leaving one st unworked.

Row 2 Sl 1, k1, ssk, k1; turn, leaving one st unworked.

Row 3 Sl 1, k2, ssk; turn.

Row 4 K3, ssk—4 sts.

Gusset

Pickup rnd On one needle, pick up and knit 5 sts along the heel flap; on a second needle, k8 instep sts; on a third needle, pick up and knit 5 sts along the other side of the heel flap, k2 from the heel flap; place a marker to indicate beg of rnd—22 sts total sts, arranged on 3 needles 7-8-7.

Rnd 1 Purl.

Rnd 2 On the first needle, knit to last 2 sts, k2tog; on the second needle, knit across the instep sts; on the third needle, ssk, knit to the end of the rnd—20 sts.

Rnd 3 Purl.

Rnds 4–5 Rep Rnds 2–3—18 sts.

Rnds 6–7 Rep Rnds 2–3—16 sts.

Cont working garter stitch in-the-round (knit 1 rnd, purl 1 rnd) until the foot measures approx $4\frac{1}{2}$" (11.4 cm) from the back of the heel.

Toe

[K2, k2tog] around—12 sts. Purl 1 rnd.

[K2tog] around—6 sts. Cut yarn.

With a yarn needle, thread the tail through the rem sts and pull tight.

Finishing

Weave in all ends.

If desired, thread elastic through the garter ridge on the inside of the bootie cuff and tie the ends together.

With this textured yarn, the garter-stitch pattern can't be seen.

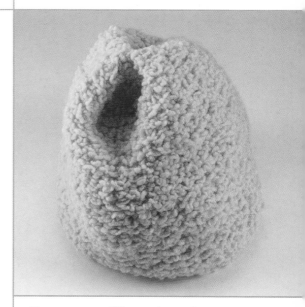

Top corners of the rectangular hat are tacked together to give it a cute shape.

Baby Cables

Design by Edie Eckman

Baby-size cables make a classic, stretchy hat—this ribbed fabric will accommodate many months of growth. The machine-washable merino wool is soft and cozy, and comes in a wide range of colors.

Baby Cables

Size: 12 months
Head circumference:
15" (38.1 cm)

YARN

4 MEDIUM Medium weight smooth yarn: approx 115 yd (105.2 m)

Shown: Kraemer Yarns' *Summit Hill;* 100% superwash merino wool; 3.5 oz (100 g) 230 yds (210.3 m):
1 ball #6359 Aquamarine

NEEDLES AND NOTIONS

One size 8 (5 mm) circular needle 16" (40 cm) long, or size needed to get gauge

Set of size 8 (5 mm) dpns, or size needed to get gauge

One stitch marker

One blunt-end yarn needle

GAUGE

22 sts and 28 rows = 4" (10 cm) in St st

33 sts and 22 rows = 4" (10 cm) in cable rib, relaxed

SPECIAL ABBREVIATIONS

RT (Right Twist) Insert the right hand needle into the second stitch on the left hand needle and knit, leaving the stitch on the needle; knit the first stitch on the left hand needle; drop both stitches off the needle.
LT (Left Twist) Insert the right hand needle behind the first stitch on the left hand needle and knit the second stitch, leaving the stitch on needle; knit the first stitch on the left hand needle; drop both stitches off the needle.

Baby cable stitch pattern

(multiple of 4 sts)
Rnds 1 and 2 [K2, p2] around.

Rnd 3 [RT, p2] around.

Rnds 4–6 Rep Rnd 1.

Rnd 7 [LT, p2] around.

Rnd 8 Rep Rnd 1.

Rep Rnds 1–8.

HAT

This hat is worked in the round. Switch to double pointed needles when the stitches no longer fit comfortably on the circular needle.

Brim

With the circular needle, CO 76 sts. Join, being careful not to twist sts. Place a marker on the needle to indicate the beg of rnd, and slip marker every rnd. Work Baby Cable patt until hat measures 5½" (14 cm) from beg, ending with Rnd 8 of patt.

Crown

Rnd 1 [K2, p2tog] around—57 sts.

Rnd 2 [K2, p1] around.

Rnd 3 [RT, p1] around.

Rnds 4–6 [K2, p1] around.

Rnd 7 [Ssk, p1] around—38 sts.

Rnd 8 [Ssk] around—19 sts.

Rnd 9 [Ssk] 9 times, k1—10 sts.

Rnd 10 [Ssk] 5 times.

Cut yarn, leaving a 6" (15.2 cm) tail.

With a yarn needle, thread the tail through the rem sts and pull tight.

Weave in all ends.

SOCK

Make two. These socks are made in the round on double pointed needles.

Cuff

With dpns, CO 24 sts. Divide the sts evenly onto three needles. Join, being careful not to twist sts. Place a marker on the needle to indicate beg of rnd, and slip marker every rnd.

First 11 rnds Work Baby Cable.

Next rnd [K2, p2] 5 times, k2, p1, slip the rem st onto the next needle.

Heel flap

Row 1 (RS) Onto one needle, p1, [k2, p2] two times, k2, p1, turn, leaving rem sts unworked—12 sts on needle.

Row 2 and all WS rows Sl 1, [p2, k2] two times, p2, k1.

Row 3 Sl 1, [LT, p2] two times, LT, p1.

Row 5 Sl 1, [k2, p2] two times, k2, p1.

Row 7 Sl 1, [RT, p2] two times, RT, p1.

Row 9 Rep Row 5.

Turn heel

Row 1 (WS) Sl 1, p7, p2tog, p1, turn, leaving remaining st unworked.

Row 2 Sl 1, k5, ssk, k1, turn, leaving remaining st unworked.

Row 3 Sl 1, p6, p2tog, turn.

Row 4 Sl 1, k6, ssk—8 sts.

No cable needles are necessary when knitting this baby cable pattern.

Gusset

On one needle, pick up and knit 7 sts along side of heel flap; on the second needle, work in established patt across 12 sts; on the third needle, pick up and knit 7 sts along side of heel flap and k4 from bottom of heel. Place a marker—this is the new beg of the rnd. Slip the rem 4 sts from bottom of heel onto the end of the first needle—total of 34 sts, arranged 11-12-11.

Rnd 1 On the first needle, knit to last 3 sts, k2tog, k1; on the second needle, work in patt; on the third needle, k1, ssk, knit to end of rnd.

Rnd 2 On the first needle, knit; on the second needle, work in patt as established; on the third needle, knit.

Rep Rnds 1 and 2 until 24 sts rem. Work 7 rnds even in established patt. Knit 1 rnd.

Decreases between the cables shape the crown of the hat.

Toe

Rnd 1 On the first needle, knit to the last 3 sts, k2tog, k1; on the second needle, k1, ssk, knit to the last 3 sts, k2tog, k1; on the third needle, k1, ssk, knit to the end of the rnd.

Rnd 2 Knit.

Rep Rnds 1 and 2 until 12 sts rem.

Rep Rnd 1–8 sts.

Knit the sts from the first needle onto the third needle.

Holding the two needles parallel, use a yarn needle to graft the toe stitches (page 93).

Socks are knit in the round from cuff to toe with cables over the instep and plain stockinette stitches on the sole.

Elf

Design by Edie Eckman

This cute combo uses slip stitches for easy two-color knitting. The short-row shaping on the instep is especially fun to knit.

Elf

Size: 12 months
Head circumference:
15" (38.1 cm)

___

YARN

[3 LIGHT] Lightweight smooth yarn (MC): approx 140 yd (128 m), (CC): approx 40 yd (36.6 m)

Shown: Plymouth Yarns *Encore DK*; 75% acrylic, 25% wool; 1.75 oz (50 g)/150 yds (137.2 m): 1 ball each #174 crimson (MC) and #256 off-white (CC)

NEEDLES AND NOTIONS

One pair size 6 (4.0 mm) needles, or size needed to get gauge

Set of size 6 (4.0 mm) dpns, or size needed to get gauge

Blunt-end yarn needle

GAUGE

22 sts and 28 rows = 4" (10 cm) in St st

Broken ridges stitch pattern

(multiple of 4 sts + 1)
Note: Slip all stitches purlwise.

Row 1 (RS) With MC, knit.

Row 2 Purl.

Row 3 With CC, k1, *k3, sl 1; rep from *, end last rep k1.

Row 4 P1, *k3, sl 1 wyif; rep from *, end last rep p1.

Row 5 With MC, k2, *sl 1, k3; rep from *, end last rep k2.

Rows 6 and 8 Purl.

Row 7 Knit.

Row 9 With CC, k2, *sl 1, k3; rep from *, end last rep k2.

Row 10 P1, k1, *sl 1 wyif, k3; rep from *, end last rep k1, p1.

Row 11 With MC, k1, *k3, sl 1; rep from *, end last rep k1.

Row 12 Purl.

Rep Rows 1–12.

Solid ridges stitch pattern

(any number)
Rows 1 and 2 With CC, knit.

Rows 3 and 5 (RS) With MC, knit.

Rows 4 and 6 With MC, purl.

Rep Rows 1–6.

HAT

This hat is worked flat, then seamed. Carry color not in use up the side of the fabric.

Brim to crown

With CC, loosely CO 81 sts.

Row 1 (WS) Knit.

Row 2 With MC, knit.

Row 3 *P2, k2; rep from *, ending with p1.

Rows 4 K1, *p2, k2; rep from *.

Rows 5–7 Cont in rib patt as established.

Work Broken Ridges patt for 20 rows, ending with Row 8.

Begin working Solid Ridges patt, and dec on Row 5, then every sixth row as follows (the decs will always occur on Row 5 of the pattern):

Dec row 1 K4, *k2 tog, k6; rep from *, ending the last rep k3—71 sts.

Dec row 2 K1, *ssk, k5; rep from * to the end of the row—61 sts.

Dec row 3 K2, *k2tog, k4; rep from *, ending the last rep k3—51 sts.

Dec row 4 K2, *ssk, k3; rep from *, ending the last rep k2—41 sts.

Dec row 5 K1, *k2tog, k2; rep from * to the end of the row—31 sts.

Dec row 6 K1, *ssk, k1; rep from * to end of row—21 sts.

Dec row 7 *K2tog; rep from *, ending with k1—11 sts.

Dec row 8 K1, [ssk] to the end of the row—6 sts.

Cut yarn, leaving a 24" (61 cm) tail for seaming. Thread yarn through the rem sts and pull tight.

Finishing

Sew the back seam.

Weave in all ends.

Slipped stitches of the broken ridges stitch pattern carry the off-white yarn up to the next row.

BOOTIES

Make two. This bootie is worked from the sole to the cuff. Parts of it are worked in the round.

Sole

With MC, CO 6 sts onto one dpn.

Row 1 K1f&b, k4, k1f&b—8 sts.

Working back and forth, knit every row until sole measures 4" (10.2 cm) from beg.

Next (Dec) row K2tog, k4, k2tog—6 sts.

Knit one row.

Foot

With a second needle, pick up and knit 22 sts along the long side of the sole; with a third needle, pick up and knit 6 sts; with a fourth needle, pick up and knit 22 sts along the other long side of the sole—56 sts.

Rnd 1 With CC, knit.

Rnd 2 Purl.

Rnds 3–5 With MC, knit.

Rnd 6 With CC, *sl 1, k3; rep from * to the end of the row.

Rnd 7 *Sl 1, k3; rep from *.

Rnd 8 With MC, *k2, sl 1, k1; rep from * to the end of the row.

Rnds 9–10 Knit.

Rnd 11 With CC, knit.

Row 12 Purl.

Rnd 13 With MC, knit.

Instep

Knit 7, turn, leaving the rem sts unworked.

*K2tog, k7, turn; rep from * until 28 sts rem. Do not turn at end of last row.

Knit 1 rnd.

Cuff

Work in k1, p1 rib for 2" (5.1 cm). BO loosely.

Finishing

Weave in all ends.

Garter-stitch sole is worked flat. Then stitches are picked up around the sole on dpns to begin working in the round.

Wiggly Stripes

Design by Edie Eckman

Nubby yarn and occasional slip-stitches turn ordinary "straight-across" stripes into ones that wave and wiggle! Choose your own colorway for a different look, or use up bits of leftover yarn for a charming scrap-yarn set.

Wiggly Stripes

Size: 12 months
Head circumference:
15" (38.1 cm)

YARN

3 Lightweight smooth yarn
LIGHT with nubs
(A): approx 40 yd (36.6 m),
(B): approx 35 yd (32 m),
(C): approx 35 yd (32 m),
(D): approx 35 yd (32 m)

Shown: Coats & Clark *TLC Wiggles*; 100% acrylic; 3.5 oz (100 g)/250 yd (228.6 m): 1 ball each #608 Blue (A), #158 Yellow (B), #727 Green (C), #209 Orange (D)

NEEDLES AND NOTIONS

One pair size 6 (4.0 mm) needles, or size needed to get gauge

Set of size 6 (4.0 mm) dpns, or size needed to get gauge

One stitch marker

One blunt-end yarn needle

GAUGE

20 sts and 30 rows = 4" (10 cm) in Slip-stitch Stripe Pattern

Slip-stitch stripe pattern

(multiple of 4 sts + 3)
Row 1 (RS) K3, *sl 1, k3; rep from * to end of row.

Row 2 Purl.

Row 3 K1, *sl 1, k3; rep from *, ending last rep k1.

Row 4 Purl.

Repeat Rows 1-4, changing colors every RS row.

HAT

This hat is worked flat, then seamed.

Brim

With A, CO 67 sts.

Work 6 rows of k1, p1 rib.

With B, begin Slip-stitch Stripe Pattern, working two rows each of B, C, D, and A.

Work five complete reps of stripe patt, then work 3 more rows of patt, ending on RS with A.

Top

Row 1 (Dec) With A, *p9, p2tog; rep from *, ending p1—61 sts.

Row 2 With B, *k1, sl 1, k2; rep from *, ending k1.

Row 3 Purl.

Row 4 With C, *k3, sl 1; rep from *, ending k1.

Row 5 (Dec) P1, *p2tog, p8; rep from * to end of row—55 sts.

Row 6 With D, *k2, sl 1, k1; rep from *, ending k3.

Row 7 Purl.

Row 8 With A, k1, *k3, sl 1, rep from *, ending k2.

Row 9 Purl.

Row 10 With B, *k2, sl 1, k1; rep from *, ending k3.

Row 11 (Dec) *P7, p2tog; rep from *, ending p1—49 sts.

Row 12 With C, *k3, sl 1; rep from *, ending k1.

Row 13 Purl.

Row 14 With D, *k1, sl 1, k2; rep from *, ending k1.

Row 15 Purl.

Row 16 With A, *k2, sl 1, k1; rep from *, ending k1.

Row 17 (Dec) *P2tog, p6; rep from *, ending p1—43 sts.

Row 18 With B, k2, *k2, sl 1, k1; rep from *, ending k1.

Row 19 Purl.

Row 20 With C, *k3, sl 1; rep from *, ending k3.

Row 21 Purl.

Row 22 With D, *k1, sl 1, k2; rep from *, ending last rep k1.

Row 23 Purl.

Row 24 With A, *k3, sl 1; rep from *, ending k3.

Row 25 Purl.

Row 26 With B, *k1, sl 1, k2; rep from *, ending last rep k1.

Row 27 (Dec) P1, *p2tog, p2; rep from *, ending p2—33 sts.

Row 28 With C, *k3, sl 1; rep from *, ending k1.

Row 29 Purl.

Row 30 With D, *k1, sl 1, k2; rep from *, ending k1.

Row 31 Purl.

Row 32 With A, rep Row 28.

Row 33 Purl.

Row 34 With B, rep Row 30.

Row 35 (Dec) P1, *p2tog, p2; rep from * to end of row—25 sts.

Row 36 With C, *k3, sl 1; rep from *, ending k1.

Row 37 Purl.

Row 38 With D, *k1, sl 1, k2; rep from *, ending k1.

Slipped stitches pull the color of one row up into the next row for a "wiggly" effect.

Row 39 (Dec) *P2tog; rep from *, ending p1—13 sts.

Row 40 With A, *k1, sl 1, k2; rep from *, ending k1.

Row 41 (Dec) *P2tog; rep from *, ending p1.

Row 42 (Dec) With A, *k2tog; rep from * to end of row—5 sts.

Cut yarn, leaving an 18" (45.7 cm) tail for sewing seam. Thread tail through rem sts and pull tight. Sew side seam.

BOOTIES

Make two. These booties are worked in the round.

Booties are worked in the round from the cuff to the center of the sole.

Cuff

With dpns and A, CO 28 sts and distribute evenly on 3 needles. Place a marker on the first needle to indicate beg of rnd, and slip marker every rnd.

Rnds 1–5 *K1, p1; rep from * around.

Rnd 6 With B, *k3, sl 1; rep from * around.

Rnd 7 Knit.

Rnd 8 With C, *k1, sl 1, k2; rep from * around.

Rnd 9 Knit.

Rnds 10 and 11 With D, rep Rnds 6 and 7.

Rnds 12 and 13 With A, rep Rnds 8 and 9.

Instep

Row 1 (RS) With B, *k3, sl 1; rep from * once more, k3; turn, leaving remaining 17 sts unworked—11 sts. Slip 17 unworked sts to one dpn for heel.

Row 2 Purl.

Row 3 With C, *k1, sl 1, k2; rep from once, k1, sl 1, k1.

Row 4 Purl.

Row 5 With D, *k3, sl 1; rep from *, once, k3.

Row 6 Purl.

Cont in Slip-stitch Stripe as established for 22 more rows, ending with a WS of C.

Cut A, B, C, and D.

Foot

Rnd 1 (pickup rnd) With RS facing, attach B and work heel sts in patt as established; with a second needle, pick up and knit 15 sts along side of instep; with a third needle, k11 toe sts; with a fourth, pick up and knit 15 sts along other side of instep. Rearrange the sts as follows: Slip the first and last 2 sts of the heel needle to the instep needles, and slip 1 st from each instep needle to the toe needle—total of 58 sts (13 heel sts, 16 instep sts, 13 toe sts, 16 instep sts).

Rnd 2 (Dec) Knit to the toe needle, k2tog, k9, ssk, knit to end—56 sts (13-16-11-16). Cut B.

Rnd 3 With C, work in Slip-stitch Stripe as established.

Rnd 4 Knit. Cut C.

Rnd 5 With D, work in Slip-stitch Stripe as established.

Rnd 6 Knit. Cut D.

Rnd 7 With A, work in Slip-stitch Stripe as established.

Sole

Rnd 1 (Dec) *Ssk, knit to last 2 sts on needle, k2tog; rep from * on each of the other 3 needles—48 sts.

Rnd 2 Knit.

Rnds 3 and 4 Rep Dec rnd—32 sts.

Rnd 5 Knit.

Rnd 6 Rep Dec rnd—24 sts.

Rnd 7 On one needle, ssk, k1, k2tog, ssk, k4, k2tog; on second needle, SK2P, ssk, k4, k2tog, k1 from heel needle—16 sts (8 sts on each needle).

Finishing

Cut yarn, leaving an 8" (20.3 cm) tail. Divide sts evenly onto two needles. Graft stitches together (page 93).

Weave in all ends.

Neon Brights

Design by Edie Eckman

Your baby will really stand out from the crowd when wearing this super-bright set! Worked back and forth, this is an easy project that is fun for both new and experienced knitters.

Neon
Size:
Hea
ap

...12 months
...d circumference:
...prox 15" (38.1 cm)

YARN

2 **FINE** Fine weight smooth yarn
(A): 115 yd (105.2 m),
(B): 18 yd (16.5 m),
(C): 12 yd (11 m),
(D): 11 yd (10 m)

Shown: Dale of Norway *Falk;*
100% machine washable wool;
1.75 oz (50 g)/116 yd (106 m):
1 ball each #018 green (A),
#0130 orange (B), #0120
yellow (C), #0144 pink (D)

NEEDLES AND NOTIONS

Three size 6 (4.0 mm)
needles, or size needed to get
gauge

One size 6 (4.0 mm) circular
needle 24" (60 cm) long, or
size needed to get gauge

Two stitch holders

One blunt-end yarn needle

GAUGE

22 sts and 36 rows = 4" (10
cm) in Seed Stitch

SPECIAL ABBREVIATION

dec2 (double decrease) Slip 2
stitches together kwise, k1, pass
the 2 slipped stitches over the k1;
this is a centered double decrease.

Seed stitch pattern

(multiple of 2 sts)
Row 1 (WS) [K1, p1] across.

Row 2 [P1, k1] across.

Rep Rows 1 and 2.

HAT

This hat is worked back and forth on a circular needle.

Brim

With the circular needle, CO 78 sts.

Work 9 rows in seed stitch.

Row 10 (RS) With B, knit.

Row 11 With B, purl. Cut B.

Row 12 With A, knit.

Work 3 rows in seed stitch.

Row 16 *K2 C, k2 D; rep from * to last 2 sts, ending with k2 C.

Row 17 *P2 C, p2 D; rep from * to last 2 sts, ending with p2 C.
Cut C and D.

Row 18 With A, knit.

Work even in seed stitch until the hat measures 4½" (11.5 cm) from beg, ending with a WS row.

Crown

Row 1 (Dec) *K9, k2tog; rep from * across, ending, k1—71 sts.

Row 2 and all WS rows Purl.

Row 3 (Dec) *K8, k2tog; rep from * across, ending k1—64 sts.

Row 5 (Dec) *K7, k2tog; rep from * across, ending k1—57 sts.

Cont to dec in this manner, working 1 fewer st before the k2tog on each succeeding Dec row, until 15 sts rem.

Next row [K2tog] across, ending k1—8 sts.

Cut yarn, leaving an 8" (20.3 cm) tail for sewing seam. Thread yarn through the rem sts and pull tight.

Finishing

Sew the back seam.

Weave in all ends.

To make the tassel, cut two 12" (30.5 cm) lengths of D and four 12" (30.5 cm) lengths of C. Tie the ends of the strands together. Braid, using like colors together, then knot the end to secure. Pull the braid through the top of the hat and tie in a knot.

BOOTIE

Make two. The bootie is worked back and forth, but the foot shaping requires that a third needle be used; this can be a double-point needle if you choose.

Cuff

With A, CO 30 sts.

Work 4 rows in seed stitch.

Row 5 (WS) Purl.

Row 6 (eyelet row) K1, *k2tog, yo, k1; rep from * across, ending k2.

Work 3 rows in seed stitch.

Row 10 With B, knit.

Row 11 With B, purl. Cut B.

Row 12 With A, knit.

Work 3 rows in seed stitch.

Instep

Work in patt across 20 sts, put the rem 10 sts on a holder, turn. Work in patt across 10 sts; put the rem 10 sts on a holder. Working on these 10 sts only, cont in patt until the instep equals approximately 2¹/₂" (6.25 cm), ending with a RS row.

Next row K2tog, work in patt across 6 sts, k2tog—8 sts. Cut A.

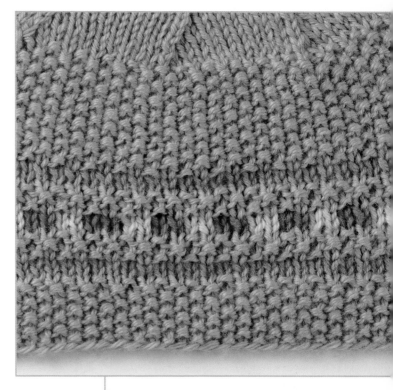

Bright stripes of color cut through the seed-stitch background.

Evenly spaced decreases shape the crown.

Foot

With RS facing, rejoin A at the center back, work in patt across the 10 sts on the holder, pick up 14 sts along the side of instep, [k1, p1] twice from the instep needle; on the second needle, [k1, p1] twice from instep needle, pick up 13 sts along the side of instep, work in patt across the rem 10 sts on the holder—55 sts.

Next row (WS) *K1, p1; rep from * across.

Cont working back and forth in established patt for 6 more rows.

Sole

Row 1 (RS) K4, dec2, k15, dec2, k6, dec2, k14, dec2, k4—47 sts.

Row 2 and all WS rows Purl.

Row 3 K3, dec2, k13, dec2, k4, dec2, k12, dec2, k3—39 sts.

Row 5 K2, dec2, k11, dec2, k2, dec2, k10, dec2, k2—31 sts.

Row 7 K1, dec2, k9, [dec2] twice, k8, dec2, k1—23 sts.

Finishing

Fold the sole in half, and holding the two needles parallel, graft the sts tog (page 93).

Sew the back seam.

Weave in all ends.

Make a braid as for the hat tie. Weave through the eyelets on the cuff and tie at the front.

Buttery Beanie

Design by Debby Ware

Your newborn will remind you of a just-hatched chick in this little yellow, white, and orange beanie. With easy-to-make bobbles and a swirly crown with a cute tip on top, this hat is a lot of fun to create. A small ruffle dresses up the booties.

Buttery Beanie

Size: Newborn to 6 months.
Head circumference:
approx 12" (30.5 cm)

___

YARN

[3 LIGHT] Lightweight smooth yarn
(A): approx 90 yd (82.3 m),
(B): approx 15 yd (13.7 m),
(C): approx 40 yd (36.6 m),
(D): approx 8 yd (7.3 m)

Shown: S.R. Kertzer *Super 10*;
100% mercerized cotton; 4.4
oz (125 g)/250 yds (228.6 m):
1 skein each of #3532 Butter
Yellow (A), #3533 Bright
Yellow (B), White (C), #3401
Orange (D)

NEEDLES AND NOTIONS

One pair size 3 (3.25 mm)
needles

One size 4 (3.5 mm) circular
needle, or size needed to get
gauge

Set of size 4 (3.5 mm) dpns,
or size needed to get gauge

One stitch marker

One blunt-end yarn needle

GAUGE

22 sts and 28 rows = 4"
(10 cm) over St st using larger
needles

Seed stitch pattern

(multiple of 2 sts)
Row 1 *K1, p1; rep from * to end of row.

Row 2 Purl each knit st and knit each purl st.

Rep Row 2.

Bobble stitch pattern

K1f&b, k1 in same st, turn; k3, turn; k2, pass the first st over the second st, k1, pass the first st over the second st.

HAT

This hat is worked in the round. Switch to double pointed needles when directed or when the stitches no longer fit comfortably on the circular needle.

Hem and side

With circular needle and A, CO 80 sts. Join, being careful not to twist sts. Place marker on needle to indicate beg of rnd, and slip marker every rnd.

Rnd 1 Purl.

Rnds 2–9 Knit.

Rnds 10 and 11 (hem rnds) Purl.

Rnd 1 Attach C. *K1 C, k1 A; rep from * to end of rnd.

Rnd 2 With C only, *K1, sl 1 pwise; rep from * to end of rnd.

Rnd 3 *K1 C, p1 A; rep from * to end of rnd.

Rnds 4–8 Rep Rnd 3.

Rnd 9 With A, knit.

Rnds 10 and 11 With A, purl. Cut A.

Rnds 12–15 With C, knit.

Rnds 16 and 17 With B, knit.

Rnd 18 *With C, make bobble (page 62), k4 B; rep from * to end of rnd.

Rnds 19 and 20 With B, knit. Cut B.

Rnds 21–28 With C, knit. Cut C.

Rnds 29–31 With A, knit 1 rnd. Purl 2 rnds.

Rnds 32 and 33 With B, knit 1 rnd, purl 1 rnd.

Swirl crown

Distribute sts evenly on 4 dpns—20 sts on each.

Next 4 rnds (Dec rnds) With A, *ssk, knit to the end of the needle; rep from * around.

Next 2 rnds With B, work Dec rnd, then purl 1 rnd with no decs—60 sts.

Rep previous 6 rnds until 8 sts rem.

Next rnd [K2tog] 5 times—3 sts rem. Put all 3 st on 1 dpn. Cut A.

Attach B and knit I-cord for approx 3½" (8.9 cm). Cut B. With D, work 4 more rows. Cut D, leaving a 6" (15.2 cm) tail. Use a yarn needle to draw tail through the remaining sts, then down into the center of the cord.

Finishing

Weave in all ends.

With D, embroider French knots (page 94) between the bobbles.

Fold the hem to the inside at the hem rnds. With a yarn needle and D, and using the photo as a guide, secure the hem edge to bottom band by weaving yarn in and out of the stitches of both pieces in evenly spaced running stitches.

Use the same method to create a welt between the sides and crown; weave the yarn in and out of the stitches on the third rows on either side of the ridge.

Tie the I-cord into a knot on top letting the tip peek out.

Running stitches (in orange) hold the hem in place and shape a welt between the sides and crown of the hat.

Decreases shape the crown into a swirl that tapers into an I-cord top knot.

BOOTIES

Make two. When casting on or cutting yarn, leave 12" (30.5 cm) tails for seaming. Each lined bootie is made from two squares that are sewn together and one square folded into a triangle; a ruffle is added to the top section.

Bottom section

Make two per bootie.

With the smaller needles and C, CO 18 sts. Work in seed stitch until you have made a perfect square. BO all sts in patt.

Place the two squares together and, using a yarn needle and C, sew the two together around the edges. Fold three corners to the center. This forms an open envelope. With a yarn needle and C, carefully sew the two resulting seams at the bootie toe.

Top section

Make one per bootie.

With the smaller needles and A, CO 24 sts. Work in garter stitch until you have made a perfect square. Fold the square diagonally to form a triangle. With a yarn needle and A, sew the edges together.

Ruffle

With B, pick up and knit approx 46-48 sts along the folded edge of the triangle.

Row 1 K1f&b in each st, doubling the number of sts you first picked up.

Row 2 (Buttonhole) K3, BO 2 sts, knit to the last 5 sts, BO 2 sts, k3.

Next Row K3, CO 2 sts over the bound off sts, knit to last 3 sts, CO 2 sts over the bound off sts, k3.

BO.

Finishing

Weave in all ends.

With the RS of the ruffle facing inward, abut the sewn edges of the triangular top section to the open edges of the envelope-shaped bottom section, matching the square corner of the triangle to the point of the "envelope flap" at the heel of the bootie. The triangle points will come together at the junction of the toe seam. Carefully sew into place.

Make a 3-st I-cord tie (page 91), approx 14" (35.6 cm) or long enough to tie into a bow. Pull the tie through the button-holes, then tie a tight knot at each end of the cord to keep it secure on the bootie. Tie it in a big bow to help keep these booties securely on your little cutie's tootsies!

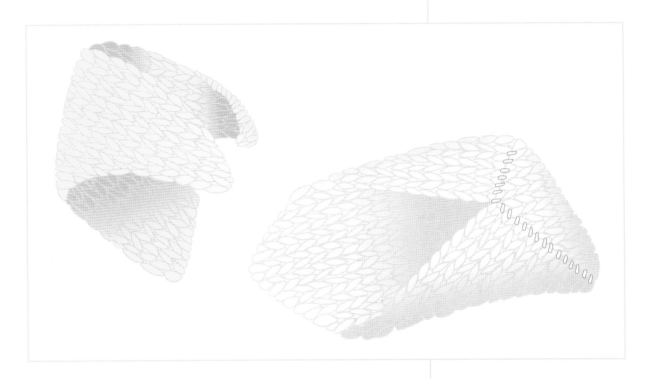

Ribbons and Bows

Design by Debby Ware

Your baby will be dressed to the nines with this ribbon-topped hat on her head. This is a simple project—just work a tube in the round, add a drawstring on top, and pull!

Ribbons and Bows

Size: 6 months to 2 years
Head circumference:
14" (35.6 cm)

YARN

3 LIGHT Lightweight smooth yarn
(A): approx 160 yd (146.3 m),
(B): approx 80 yd (73.4 m),
(C): approx 90 yd (82.3 m),
(D): approx 10 yd (9.1 m)

Shown: S.R. Kertzer *Super 10;*
100% mercerized cotton; 4.4 oz
(125 g)/250 yd (228.6 m):
1 skein each of #3882
Periwinkle (A), #3724 Lime (B),
#3553 Canary (C), #3454
Bubblegum (D)

4 MEDIUM Medium weight novelty
yarn tufted with ribbons and
eyelash (E): approx 60 yds
(54.9 m)

Shown: Trendsetter *JOY;* 75%
nylon, 25% polyester;
0.88 oz (25 g)/65 yd (59.4 m):
1 skein #1194

NEEDLES AND NOTIONS

One pair size 3 (3.25 mm)
knitting needles

One size 4 (3.5 mm) circular
needle 16" (40 cm) long, or
size needed to get gauge

Two small stitch holders

One blunt-end yarn needle

GAUGE

22 sts and 28 rows = 4"
(10 cm) over St st using cotton
yarn

Seed stitch pattern

(multiple of 2 sts)
Row 1 *K1, p1; rep from * to end of row.

Row 2 Purl each knit st and knit each purl st.

Rep Row 2.

HAT

This hat is worked in the round.

Brim

With circular needle and C, CO 90 sts. Join, being careful not to twist sts. Place a marker on the needle to indicate the beg of rnd, and slip marker every rnd.

Rnd 1 Purl.

Rnd 2 Attach A. *K1, sl 1 wyib; rep from * to end of rnd.

Rnd 3 With A, *p1, sl 1 wyib; rep from * to end of rnd.

Rnd 4 With C, knit.

Rnd 5 With C, purl.

Rnd 6 Attach B. Rep Rnd 2.

Rnds 7–9 With B, rep Rnds 3 thru 5.

Rnds 10–14 With A, then C, rep Rnds 2-5. Cut C.

Next 2 rnds With B, knit one rnd, then purl one rnd.

Next 5 rnds With A, knit.

Rep previous 7 rnds 4 more times. Cut B.

Next 2 rnds Attach D. Knit 1 rnd, then purl 1 rnd.

Next rnd With A, knit.

Next rnd (Eyelet rnd) With A, *k4, yo, k2tog; rep from * to end of rnd.

Next rnd With A, knit.

Next 2 rnds With D, knit 1 rnd, then purl 1 rnd. Cut D.

Attach E and, holding A and E together, work seed st for 2" (5 cm). Cut E.

With A, BO all sts. Cut A.

Finishing

Weave in all ends.

Using a yarn needle, carefully poke and pull all those little ribbon ends that have ended up on the inside of the hat to the outside.

Make a 3-st I-cord tie (page 91), approx 22" (55.9 cm) long. Weave the tie through the eyelets. Make a knot at each end of the cord to keep it from slipping out of the eyelets. Tie in a big bow.

BOOTIES

Make two. These booties are worked flat from the cuff down, then seamed.

Cuff

With smaller needles and A, CO 36 sts.

First 3 rows Attach E and holding A and E together, work in seed stitch. Cut E.

Next 2 rows With A, knit 1 row, then purl 1 row.

Next row (Eyelet row) K2, *yo, k2tog, k4*; rep from * to last 4 sts, ending last rep yo, k2tog, k2.

Next row Purl.

Next 7 rows Work k2, p1 rib.

Instep

Next row (WS) K24, turn. Put the 12 unworked sts on a holder.

Next row Attach B. K12, turn. Put the 12 unworked sts on a second holder.

Next 12 rows Work in seed stitch on these 12 sts only. Cut B.

Hat is knitted flat and then sewn into a tube. A drawstring gathers the top into a riot of ribbons.

Slipped stitches carry the yellow yarn into the periwinkle and green rows to give the brim band a checkered look.

Foot

Next row With RS facing, attach C at the center back, knit 12 sts from the holder, pick up and knit 10 sts along the side of the instep, k12 on instep needle, pick up and knit 10 sts along the other side of the instep, knit 12 sts from the other holder—56 sts.

Next 4 rows With C, knit.

Next row (make welt) With WS facing, *slip the first st from the left-hand to the right-hand needle. Count 3 ridges down on the WS of garter st rows; pick up and knit the top loop of the first st on this ridge, pass the slipped st over the new st; rep from * to the end of the row. (See page 92 for step-by-step photos.)

Next 8 rows Attach A. Knit.
Cut A.

Next 2 rows With C, knit. Cut C.

Shape sole

With RS facing, slip first 22 sts onto right hand needle. Attach B and k12 sts, turn. *K11, k2tog (i.e. knit 1 A and 1 C tog), turn; rep from * until all C sts are worked—12 sts rem on needle. K2tog across the row.

Cut yarn leaving a 6" (15.2 cm) tail and, with a yarn needle, pass the tail through the sts on needle and pull tight.

Finishing

Pull "ribbons" to RS of booties as for hat.

Sew the back seam.

Weave in all ends.

With B, make a 3-st I-cord tie (page 91) 18" (45.7 cm) long. Weave the tie through the eyelets and knot each end to keep the cord from slipping through eyelets. Tie in a bow.

A knitted welt (yellow) defines and shapes the top of the bootie.

Flowers and Fluff

Design by Debby Ware

Is your baby a girly girl? She'll be *très jolie* wearing this flower-strewn beret! The simple-to-knit roses are sewn on after the set is complete.

Flowers and Fluff

Size: 6 months to 2 years
Head circumference:
16" (40.6 cm)

___

YARN

(3 LIGHT) Lightweight smooth yarn
(A): approx 130 yd (18.9 m),
(B): approx 60 yd (54.9 m),
(C): approx 80 yd (73.2 m),
(D): approx 20 yd (18.3 m)

Shown: S.R. Kertzer *Super 10*;
100% mercerized cotton; 4.4 oz
(125 g)/250 yd (228.6 m):
1 skein each #3454 Bubblegum
(A), 3443 Palek Pink (B,) #3535
Key Lime (C), #3401 Orange (D)

(4 MEDIUM) Medium weight eyelash
yarn (E): approx 65 yds (59.4 m)

Shown: Trendsetter *Willow;* 100%
polyester; 1.75 oz (50 g)/65 yd
(59.4 m): 1 skein #25 (E)

NEEDLES AND NOTIONS

One pair size 3 (3.25 mm)
knitting needles

One size 4 (3.5 mm) circular
needle 16" (40 cm) long, or size
needed to get gauge

Set of size 4 (3.5 mm) dpns, or
size needed to get gauge

Four stitch markers, one in
a different color to indicate
beg of rnd

Two small stitch holders

One blunt-end yarn needle

GAUGE

22 sts and 28 rows = 4" (10
cm) over St st using larger
needles

Seed stitch pattern

(multiple of 2 sts)
Row 1 *K1, p1; rep from * to end of row.

Row 2 Purl each knit stitch, and knit each purl stitch.
Rep Row 2.

HAT

This hat is worked in the round. Switch to double pointed needles when the stitches no longer fit comfortably on the circular needle.

Brim

With circular needle and A, CO 80 sts. Join, being careful not to twist sts. Place a marker on the needle to indicate the beg of rnd, and slip marker every rnd.

Rnd 1 Purl.

Rnds 2–7 Attach B and work k1, p1 rib. Cut B.

Rnds 8 and 9 With A, knit 1 rnd, purl 1 rnd. Cut A.

Rnds 10 and 11 Attach D. Knit 1 rnd, purl 1 rnd.

Rnd 12 Attach C. Knit 1 rnd, placing a marker every 20 sts.

Rnds 13–16 With C, *k1, k1f&b, knit to 1 st before marker, k1f&b, slip marker; rep from * around—112 sts.

Rnds 17 and 18 With D, knit 1 rnd, purl 1 rnd.

Rnds 19–22 With C, rep Rnds 13–16—144 sts (36 sts between each marker). Cut C.

Rnds 23 and 24 With D, knit 1 rnd, purl 1 rnd. Cut D.

Rnds 25 and 26 Attach E. Purl. Cut E.

Rnd 27 Attach A and knit.

Swirl top

Next (Dec) rnd With A, *ssk, knit to next marker; rep from * to end of rnd—140 sts.

Rep Dec rnd every rnd until 12 sts rem.

Next rnd *K2tog; rep from * around—6 sts.

Cut yarn, leaving a 6" (15.2 cm) tail.

With a yarn needle, thread the tail through the rem sts and pull tight.

Small rose

With larger needles and B, CO 14 sts.

Row 1 *K1f&b in first st; rep from * to the end of the row—28 sts.

BO pwise, leaving an 8" (20.3 cm) tail. Curl the strip into a tight spiral to create rose, and using the tail, tack the bottom together. Use the CO and BO tails to sew the rose to the hat.

Large rose

With larger needles and C, CO 10 sts.

Row 1 (RS) Knit.

Row 2 and all WS rows Purl.

Row 3 *K1f&b; rep from * to end—20 sts.

Rows 5, 7, and 9 Rep Row 3—160 sts.

BO pwise, leaving an 8" (20.3 cm) tail. Curl the strip into a tight spiral to create rose, and using the tail, tack the bottom together. Use the CO and BO tails to sew the rose to the hat.

Finishing

Weave in all ends.

With C, make one large rose and attach to the peak of
the beret.

With B, embroider a 6-wrap French knot (page 94) in the center of the large rose.

With B, make 8 small roses. Attach two to each section of the underside of the beret, carefully centering each.

With C, embroider a 3-wrap French knot (page 94) in the center of each small rose.

Small roses with French-knot centers adorn the underside of the beret.

Decrease rows square off the beret top in a soft swirl.

BOOTIES

Make two. These booties are worked flat from the cuff down, then seamed.

Cuff

With smaller needles and E, CO 36 sts.

Next 4 rows With E, purl. Cut E.

Next 8 rows Attach D. Work in seed stitch.

Next (eyelet) row K2, *yo, k2tog, k4; rep from *, ending last rep k2.

Next row Work in seed stitch.

Instep

Next row (WS) K24, turn. Put the 12 unworked sts on a holder.

Next row Attach A. K12, turn. Put the 12 unworked sts on a second holder.

Next 12 rows Work in seed stitch on these 12 sts only. Cut A.

Foot

Next row With RS facing, attach C at the center back, knit 12 sts from the holder, pick up and knit 10 sts along the side of the instep, k12 on instep needle, pick up and knit 10 sts along the other side of the instep, knit 12 sts from the other holder—56 sts.

Next 4 rows With C, knit.

Next row (make welt) With WS facing, *slip the first st from the left-hand to the right-hand needle. Count 3 ridges down on the WS of garter st rows; pick up and knit the top loop of the first st on this ridge, pass the slipped st over the new st; rep from * to the end of the row. (See page 92 for step-by-step photos.)

Next 8 rows Attach E. Knit. Cut E.

Next 2 rows With C, knit. Cut C.

Sole

With RS facing, slip first 22 sts onto right hand needle. Attach A and D. With A, k12, turn.

Next (joining) row K11, k2tog (i.e. knit 1 A and 1 C tog), turn. With D, rep last row twice. Cont working joining row, alternating A and D, until all C sts are worked—12 sts rem on needle. K2tog across the row.

Cut yarn leaving a 6" (15.2 cm) tail and, with a yarn needle, pass the tail through the sts on needle and pull tight.

Finishing

Weave in all loose ends.

Sew back seam.

With B, make a small rose and attach to the top of the bootie.

With C, embroider a 3-wrap French knot (page 94) in the middle of the rose.

With smaller needles, make a 3-st I-cord (page 91), approx 18" (45.7 cm) long. Weave the cord through the eyelets, then tie in a big bow.

Sam the Man

Design by Debby Ware

Hi! I'm Sam the Man! With red ears and nose, blue eyes and green hair, I'll be your baby's most colorful friend! The best thing is that I'm very easy to make—sew on a couple bobbles and several I-cords and voilà, I have a face!

Sam the Man

Size: 6 to 18 Months
Head circumference: 15" (38.1 cm)

YARN

(3) LIGHT Lightweight smooth yarn
(A): approx 200 yd (182.9 m),
(B): approx 2 yd (1.8 m),
(C): approx 75 yd (68.6 m),
(D): approx 25 yd (22.9 m),
(E): 3 yd (2.7 m),
(F): 2 yd (1.8 m)

Shown: S.R. Kertzer *Super 10*;
100% mercerized cotton; 4.4 oz
(125 g)/250 yds (228.6 m):
1 skein each #3358 Ginger (A),
#3454 Bubblegum (B), #3997
Frankly Scarlet (C), #3535 Key
Lime (D), #3062 Azure (E),
Black (F)

NEEDLES AND NOTIONS

One pair size 3 (3.25 mm)
knitting needles

One size 4 (3.5 mm) circular
needle 16" (40 cm) long, or
size needed to get gauge

Set of size 4 (3.5 mm) dpns, or
size to get gauge

One stitch marker

One blunt-end yarn needle

GAUGE

22 sts and 29 rows = 4"
(10 cm) over St st using larger
needles

Seed stitch pattern

(multiple of 2 sts)
Row 1 *K1, p1; rep from * to end of row.

Row 2 Purl each knit st and knit each purl st.

Rep Row 2.

HAT

This hat is worked in the round. Switch to double pointed needles when the stitches no longer fit comfortably on the circular needle.

Brim to crown

With circular needle and A, CO 90 sts. Join, being careful not to twist sts. Place marker on needle to indicate beg of rnd, and slip marker every rnd.

Rnd 1 Purl.

Rnd 2 Attach C. *K1, sl 1; rep from * to end of rnd.

Rnd 3 With C, *p1, sl 1; rep from * to end of rnd.

Rnd 4 With A, knit.

Rnd 5 With A, purl.

Rep Rnds 2–5 two times more for a total of 3 ridges.

Next 10 rnds Work seed stitch.

Next (Dec) rnd *K8, k2tog; rep from * to end of rnd.

Rep the last 11 rnds 8 times more, working one fewer st between decs on each Dec rnd—9 sts.

Next rnd [K2tog] 4 times, k1—5 sts.

Cut yarn, leaving a 15" (38.1 cm) tail.

Using a yarn needle, thread the tail through the 5 sts on the needle. Pull yarn, gathering all sts tightly together.

Tie off yarn securely on WS of hat.

Embellish as instructed on pages 81, 82, and 83.

BOOTIES

Make two. When casting on or cutting yarn, leave 12" (30.5 cm) tails for seaming. These lined booties are made from folded squares which are sewn together.

Bottom section and lining

With smaller needles and A, CO 24 sts. Work in seed stitch until you have made a perfect square for the bottom. BO all sts in patt.

With smaller needles and C, CO 24 sts and work another square for the lining as above. Put one square on top of the other and, using a yarn needle and A, sew the two together around the edges. With the lining on top, fold three corners of the square to the center. This forms an open envelope with a red lining. With a yarn needle and A, carefully sew the two resulting seams at the bootie toe.

Top section

With smaller needles and A, CO 30 sts. Work in garter stitch until you have made a perfect square. Fold the square diagonally to form a triangle. With a yarn needle and A, sew the edges together.

Finishing

Abut the sewn edges of the garter st triangle and the edges of the open end of the seed st envelope, matching the square corner of the triangle at the point of the "envelope flap" at the heel of the bootie. Triangle points will come together at the junction of the toe seams. Carefully sew into place. (See illustration on page 65.)

EMBELLISHMENTS

Leave CO and BO tails at least 6" (15.2 cm) long for sewing on.

Bootie tie

Make two. Knit a 2-st I-cord (page 91), approx 5" (12.7k cm) long.

Rows of seed stitch are separated by knitted decrease rows to shape the hat.

Nose

Make three. Knit a 4-st I-cord (page 91), 2" (5.1 cm) long.

Hair

Make six or more. Knit 2-st I-cords (page 91), each approx 3" (7.6 cm) long.

Bobble eyeballs

With smaller needles and E, CO one st.

Row 1 (K1f&b) 3 times—6 sts.

Rows 2 and 4 Purl.

Rows 3 and 5 Knit.

Row 6 (P2tog) 3 times—3 sts.

Row 7 SK2P—1 st. BO.

With B, make a small French knot (page 94) in the center of each bobble.

Knot cast on and bind off tails together, creating an eyeball with a pink iris.

Bootie ears

Make four. With smaller needles and C, CO 4 sts.

Row 1 Knit.

Row 2 (Inc row) K1f&b, k to last st, k1f&b—6 sts.

Rep these two rows twice more—10 sts.

Knit 3 rows, then BO.

Here's Sam with his face all in place, right up to his I-cord hair.

Hat ears

Make two. Work same as the bootie ears, except cont working Inc row until there are 20 sts. Knit 3 rows, then BO.

Using the photographs as a guide, sew eyeballs, nose, and ears into place on each bootie and hat. Using a yarn needle and F, create running sts for a smiling mouth on each bootie and the hat. Sew I-cord hair into place on peak of hat. Thread I-cord tie through triangle points of bootie and tie a small knot.

Weave in all ends.

Dots and Ruffles

Design by Debby Ware

This extraordinary hat-and-bootie set is more challenging to knit but it's worth it. Baby will be the center of attention whenever she wears this sweet concoction!

Seed stitch pattern

Row 1 *K1, p1; rep from * to end of row.
Row 2 Purl each knit stitch and knit each purl stitch.
Rep Row 2.

HAT

This hat is worked in the round. Switch to double pointed needles when the stitches no longer fit comfortably on the circular needle.

Brim

With circular needle and B, cast on 90 sts. Join, being careful not to twist sts. Place a marker on the needle to indicate the beg of rnd, and slip the marker every rnd.

Rnd 1 Purl.

Rnd 2 Attach A. *K1 B, k1 A; rep from * to the end of the rnd.

Rnd 3 With B, *k1, sl 1; rep from * to the end of the rnd.

Rnds 4–12 *K1 B, p1 A; rep from * to the end of the rnd. Cut A.

Rnds 13 and 14 With B, knit one rnd, then purl one rnd.

Ruffle

Next (Inc) rnd *K2, k1f&b; rep from * to the end of the rnd—120 sts.

With B, work seed stitch for 2¼" (5.7 cm). Cut B.

Next rnd Attach A. Knit 1 rnd, then BO all sts pwise.

Crown

Holding the hat with RS facing, bend the ruffle down toward you and expose the join between bottom of the ruffle and the top of the ribbing. With C, pick up and knit 1 st in each "upward" loop at this join—90 sts. With C, work in St st for 2¼" (5.7 cm), or until you have "cleared" the top of the ruffle.

Next (Dec setup) rnd *K8, k2tog, pm; rep from * around—81 sts.

Knit 4 rnds.

Next (Dec) rnd *K to 2 sts before the marker, k2tog; rep from * around—72 sts.

Rep the Dec rnd every fifth rnd twice more, then every fourth rnd once, every third rnd once and every second rnd once, removing the dec markers on the last rnd—18 sts rem.

K2tog until 6 sts rem.

Cut yarn, leaving a 6" (15.2 cm) tail. Using a yarn needle, thread the tail through the rem sts on the needles. Pull the yarn, gathering sts tightly together, then secure the tail on the WS of hat.

Pom-pom

Make one pom-pom using all 3 colors of hat. Wrap the three yarns around a 3" (7.6 cm) piece of cardboard 50 to 60 times. Cut a 12" (30.5 cm) strand of A. Slip the loops off the cardboard and use the strand of yarn to tie a very tight knot around the loops. Cut through the loops of yarn on either side of the tied knot, and shake the pom-pom hard to fluff it out. Trim the ends evenly.

Finishing

With B, embroider 3-wrap French knots (page 94) all around crown, spaced as desired.

Attach the pom-pom to the peak of the hat.

Weave in all ends.

With C, embroider French knots evenly spaced around, going through both the ruffle and crown fabric, thereby attaching the ruffle to the lower portion of the crown and creating "pockets."

Two-color ribbing makes a snug brim.

Evenly spaced French knots secure the ruffle to the sides of the hat forming little pockets.

BOOTIES

These booties are knitted flat from the cuff down, then seamed. For ease in working, a third needle can be used for the first several rows of the foot shaping; this can be a double-pointed needle if you choose.

Cuff

With smaller needles and A, CO 41 sts. Cut A.

Next 8 rows Attach B, and work in k1, p1 rib. Cut B.

Work k1, p1 ribbing for 8 rows. Cut B.

Next (eyelet) row Attach A. K2, *yo, k2tog, k4; rep from * to last 3 sts, ending last rep yo, k2tog, k1.

Next row (WS) With A, purl 1 row. Cut A.

Next 6 rows Attach C, and work in St st.

Instep

Next row K28, turn. Put the 13 unworked sts on a holder.

Next row P15, turn. Put the 13 unworked sts on another holder.

Next 8 rows Work in St st on these 15 sts only. Cut C.

Foot

Next row With RS facing, attach B at the center back, knit 13 sts from holder, pick up and knit 7 sts along the side of the instep, k15 on instep needle, pick up and knit 7 sts along the other side of instep, knit 13 sts from other holder—55 sts.

Next 10 rows Work in garter stitch for 10 rows.

Welt

Next row (make welt) With WS facing, *slip the first st from the left-hand to the right-hand needle. Count 3 ridges down on the WS of garter st rows; pick up and knit the top loop of the first st on this ridge, pass the slipped st over the new st; rep from * to the end of the row. (See page 92 for step-by-step photos.)

Cut B and attach A.

Sole

Next row (RS) K27, pm, k28.

Next 5 rows Knit to marker, slip marker, k2tog, knit to end—50 sts rem.

BO.

Finishing

With B, make 10 small French knots (page 94) on top of instep of each bootie.

Sew the sole and back seams.

Weave in all ends.

Knit a 3-st I-cord tie (page 91), approx 22" (55.9 cm) long. Thread the I-cord tie through the eyelets. Make a small knot at each end of the tie to keep it from slipping out.

Special Skills

Here are some skills and techniques that are used in several projects in the book. If you are not familiar with them or need to refresh your memory, follow these directions and photos.

Circular needle

Some of the projects in this book are knit in the round using a circular needle or a set of double-pointed needles. Sometimes you will start a hat on a circular needle and then switch to double-pointed needles in the crown when fewer stitches make the work too small to fit on the circular needle. The knitting is worked from the right side in a continuous spiral, so there are no seams.

Circular needles are simply two short needles joined by a cable. The needles come in the same standard sizes as straight needles and in several different lengths. Choose a needle about 2" (5 cm) shorter than the circumference of your project, so the stitches will fit comfortably on the needle without stretching.

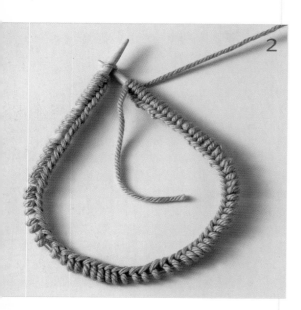

1. Cast on the number of stitches needed. Hold the needle tip with the last cast-on stitch in your right hand and the tip with the first cast-on stitch in your left hand. Make sure the cast-on edge is facing the center of the circle and is not twisted before taking your first stitch.

2. Knit the first stitch, pulling the yarn firmly to avoid a gap.

3. Continue knitting the stitches, sliding them off the needle tip and onto the cable as you go around. When you reach your cast-on tail again, you have completed the first round.

4. Slip a stitch marker onto the right-hand needle tip and continue knitting the second round. Slip the marker from tip to tip after each round.

Double-pointed needles

Double-pointed needles come in sets of four or more. Stitches are cast on continuously from one needle to the next. One needle is used to knit off the stitches that are divided among the other needles. As the last stitch is knitted off a needle, that needle then becomes the working needle.

1. Cast on the stitches onto one needle and then divide them equally or as directed in the project directions among three needles. Arrange the needles in a triangle with the first cast-on stitch on the left and the last cast-on stitch on the right. Make sure the cast-on edges are all facing the center of the triangle and are not twisted.

2. Using the fourth needle, knit the first stitch of the first needle (first cast-on stitch), pulling the yarn firmly to avoid a gap (top).

3. Continue knitting the stitches off the first needle. When the first needle is empty, use it to knit the stitches off the second needle, and so on. When you reach your cast-on tail again, you have completed the first round.

4. Slip a split-coil stitch marker after the last stitch, pulling the yarn through the marker to hold it in place (a solid ring marker will fall off the needle tip). Slip the marker after each round.

I-cord

Narrow knitted tubes, called I-cords, are so useful for tying little booties on Baby's tootsies or for tying a hat in place under a plump chin. They can also be used for embellishments, such as the nose and hair on *Sam the Man* (page 78).

1. Cast on the number of stitches needed (usually 2 to 4).

2. Knit the stitches, but do not turn.

3. Slip the stitches from the right-hand needle back to the left hand needle. (If using double-pointed needles, leave the stitches on the same needle and slide them to the other end.)

4. Bring the yarn across the back of the stitches and pull tight. Knit the next row (middle).

5. Repeat steps 3 and 4 until the cord is the desired length.

6. Break the yarn, leaving a 6" (15.2 cm) tail. Use a yarn needle to draw the tail through the remaining stitches.

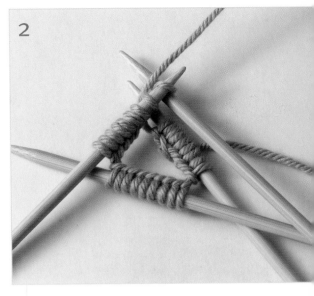

Knitted welt

Raised ridges, or welts, add a decorative element to a project, and they can also be used to emphasize a design line, such as the dividing line between the sides and crown of a hat or the rim of a bootie sole. With this method, the welt is created as you knit.

1. With wrong side facing, slip the first stitch from the left-hand to the right-hand needle.

2. Count 3 ridges down on the wrong side of the rows; pick up and knit the top loop of the first stitch on this ridge.

3. Pass the slipped stitch over the new stitch.

4. Repeat steps 1 to 3 for every stitch in the welt row.

Grafting

Grafting, also called kitchener stitch, weaves together two rows of "live" stitches (not bound off), resulting in an invisible joining. Using a yarn needle, you stitch the rows together, following the path of the stitches.

1. Cut the working yarn, leaving a tail about 18" (46 cm) long. Leave the stitches on the needles; there should be the same number of stitches on each. Hold the needles side by side in the left hand, with the right side facing up. Slide the stitches toward the needle tips.

2. The working yarn will be coming from the first stitch on the back needle. To help explain the steps, we have used a contrasting yarn as the working yarm. Thread the yarn tail on a yarn needle. Draw the yarn through the first stitch on the front needle as if to purl, and leave the stitch on the needle.

3. Keeping the yarn under the needles, draw the yarn through the first stitch on the back needle as if to knit, and leave the stitch on the needle.

4. Draw the yarn through the first stitch on the front needle as if to knit, and slip the stitch off the needle.

5. Draw the yarn through the next stitch on the front needle as if to purl, and leave the stitch on the needle.

6. Draw the yarn through the first stitch on the back needle as if to purl, and slip the stitch off the needle.

7. Draw the yarn through the next stitch on the back needle as if to knit, and leave the stitch on the needle.

8. Repeat steps 4 to 7 until all the stitches have been worked off the needles.

9. If necessary, use the tip of the yarn needle to adjust the tension of the grafting stitches until the join is invisible. With practice, your grafting will need very little adjustment.

10. Draw the yarn to the wrong side and weave in the tail end.

French knot

A technique borrowed from embroidery, French knots add interesting texture to the surface of your knitting.

1. Thread a yarn needle with appropriate yarn. Bring the needle up from the wrong side at the point where you wish to place a French knot.

3. Holding the yarn down with your left thumb, wind the yarn 3 times around the needle (up to 6 times for a large knot). Still holding the yarn firmly, twist the needle back to the starting point and insert it close to where the yarn first emerged (straddle at least one stitch).

3. Pull the yarn through to the wrong side. Secure each knot on the wrong side.

Abbreviations

approx approximately

beg begin(ning)

BO bind off

CC contrasting color

cm centimeters

CO cast on

cont continue

dec decrease

dpn double-pointed needle(s)

g grams

inc increase

k knit

k1f&b knit into front and back loop of same stitch

k2tog knit two stitches together

kwise knitwise

MC main color

M1 increase 1 by inserting the left hand needle under the horizontal thread between the stitch just worked and the next st; knit into the back of the resulting loop to make a stitch

mm millimeters

p purl

p1f&b purl into front and back loop of same stitch

p2tog purl two stitches together

patt pattern

pm place marker

psso pass slipped st over

pwise purlwise

rem remain(ing)

rep repeat

rib ribbing

rnd(s) rounds

RS right side

SK2P slip 1, k2tog, pass slipped st over (a left leaning double decrease)

sl slip

ssk slip the first and second stitches one at a time kwise, then insert left hand needle into the fronts of these stitches and knit them together

ssp slip first and second stitches one at a time kwise, then slip them back to the left hand needle; insert the right hand needle through the back loops of the two stitches (going into the second stitch first), then purl them together

st(s) stitch(es)

St st Stockinette stitch (k on RS, p on WS)

tbl through back loop

WS wrong side

wyib with yarn in back

wyif with yarn in front

yo yarn over needle

* repeat from *

[] repeat instructions in brackets as directed

About the Designers

Edie Eckman

Edie Eckman has her hands in many aspects of the fiber arts—teaching, writing, designing, and editing. Her designs are contemporary classics, accessible to the average knitter, and have appeared in many yarn company publications, magazines, and pattern leaflets. Edie travels extensively teaching at conventions, yarn shops, and guilds. She enjoys sharing in that "aha!" moment when her students grasp a new technique. Edie is the author of *The Crochet Answer Book*. Visit Edie's website: www.edieeckman.com.

Bonnie Franz

When she was only five, Bonnie Franz learned to knit from her mother. After making a blanket for her doll, she dropped the needles until her college years when she re-learned the basics and went beyond. She eventually progressed through the Master level of the Knitting Guild of America program and began designing her own patterns, which have been published in many books, booklets, magazines, and newsletters. In 2002, Bonnie started a newsletter called *Stranded* to create a forum for colorwork discussion, history, and designs. She is the author of *Double Exposure: Knit it Basic, Knit it Bold*. See more of Bonnie's designs on her website: www.bonniefranz.com.

Debby Ware

Debby Ware is a graduate of The School of Visual Arts in New York City. For many years, she sold her one-of-a-kind knit goods from her businesses and home on Martha's Vineyard. When she and her husband and son moved from the ocean to the mountains of Virginia, she started designing and producing kits for Debby Ware Knitwares. Debby is the author of *Too Cute!* See more of Debby's designs on her website: www.debbyware.com.